Light Forms

Architectural Images of Greece

Carolyn Johnson

Introduction by Kathleen Douglas

SWC EDITIONS
PUBLISHERS-LOS ANGELES

ISBN 0-9713154-6-9

Library of Congress Control Number: 2002109142

First Edition

Printed in Los Angeles by FINE ARTS PRINTING 866.480.0550

SWC EDITIONS

PUBLISHERS-LOS ANGELES

3940 Laurel Canyon Boulevard #698
Studio City, CA 91604
323.654.9339
www.stevenwaynecompany.com

IN APPRECIATION

This book is dedicated to my late father, Harvol C. Johnson, who shared my interest in photography and whose camera I used to capture these images.

I would also like to express my appreciation to Washington photographer Charles Rumph, who led the group trip to Greece that resulted in these images.

Cover Photo: ***Picasso-like Wall***
1996
Santorini

"What else is there in architecture when you talk about form and space? It is the play between the solids and the voids. Therefore, the effect of light on those solids and voids is so important. And there you cannot separate architecture from painting or sculpture. It was never more graphically evident than in Picasso's work."

I. M. Pei, architect

Light Forms

Architectual Images of Greece

Introduction by Kathleen Douglas

What is most striking about Carolyn Johnson's photographs is that they don't look like photographs. They look like abstract paintings. The viewer is engaged—he has to think about what he is seeing. It is only upon close scrutiny of her images that one realizes that they are paintings created with a photographic medium—enlargements printed from 35mm slides. She uses her lens like a surgeon's knife, excising an abstraction from the whole while capturing the tri-dimensional interplay of shadow, light and color—the results are arresting.

So skillfully has Johnson embraced the abstract forms and the dazzling light, the brilliant whites, and the stonewash and creten blues that the parent forms pale. What remains are intellectually intriguing compositions of color and shape that evoke feelings of intimacy, expectation, beauty and quiet. They speak to the soul, making you wish you were there, having that moment, knowing that clarity, feeling the mystery and absorbing the sheer beauty. While powerful, her compositions remain intimate in some way—like a whispered suggestion, a suggestion that inspires warmth, tranquility and an affinity with the light.

Johnson admits that her own affinity with light was so much a part of her that it is only in retrospect that she came to realize the strong influences of her youth. Growing up in Oklahoma, Carolyn Johnson was accustomed to the crystal clear light that saturated the glowing wheatfields and accented cerulean skies that stretched into infinity. She paid little mind to the evening and early morning transilluminations that reverberated across the skies. Perhaps she didn't always notice the lazy afternoon light that moved from golden saffron, dropping its crimson source into the horizon and leaving behind a wake of glowing amber and fuchsia to escort in the cobalt night ceiling. It is only in hindsight, that she recognized that growing up in that light captured her imagination and shaped her perceptions with razor sharp intensity.

That same intensity translated into her work as a theater photographer. Her photography reflected her unique ability to identify and capture a sheer moment of emotion that would speak to the "essence" of the performance. It was that same laser clarity of "essence" combined with her passion for architectural form that emerged from her photographic work in the Cyclades in 1996.

Greece, and the elegant simplicity of its architectural order, has captured the hearts and minds of artists for thousands of years. Johnson turned her lens, not to the capitals with spiral volutes that adorned the Parthenon nor the slender shafts and elegant bases of the Acropolis but to the forms and colors of the white washed villages of Santorini, Syros and Mykonos. Perhaps pop artist Roy Lichtenstein shared this vision when he observed that architecture is the result of the forming. In a 1983 interview he opined, " It is the kinesthetic and visual sense of position and wholeness that puts the thing into the realm of art."

Johnson's images reveal the clear influence of two masters whom she admires: I. M. Pei, whose large abstract forms and sharp geometric designs sprang from the modernist movement, and Georgia O'Keeffe, whose images seduced from the ordinary a bold new style by changing how we view things. Johnson's compositions present the viewer with a new perspective, coaxing a new visual and presenting a form "in a different light". Like the surgeon she probes her lens into the vortex of a form and so engages the viewer as to cause a new vision—her vision. Through her images Johnson takes the hand of the viewer and says, "Walk with me, come see—come see what I see."

Kathleen A. Douglas

Kathleen A. Douglas is a writer and photojournalist. As a freelancer for Associated Press, she has had her work published by the Boston Globe and many other member newspapers. She earned a Master's degree in journalism from Boston University; she continued her studies in fine art photography at the New England School of Photography and has studied under several master photographers. The spectrum of her work includes documentary and fine art photography. As a travel writer and photographer she has traveled extensively in Africa, Cuba, Haiti, Europe, Asia and Australia. She works out of her studio in Boston's North End.

"...one can create great spatial complexity through juxtaposition and combination."

I. M. Pei, architect

Puzzle Pieces — 1

1996

Santorini

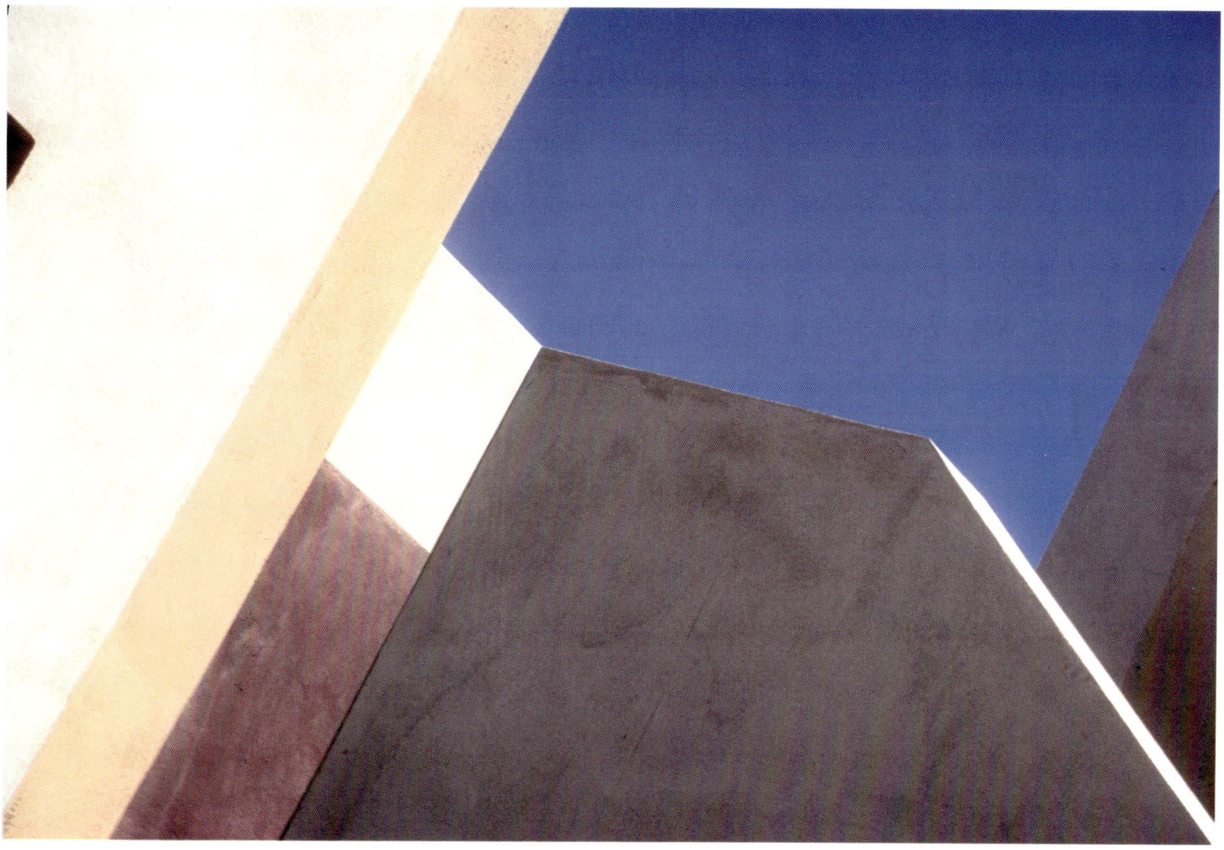

"...the relation between what we see and what we know is never settled."

John Berger, art critic

Gray Zig Zags
1996
Santorini

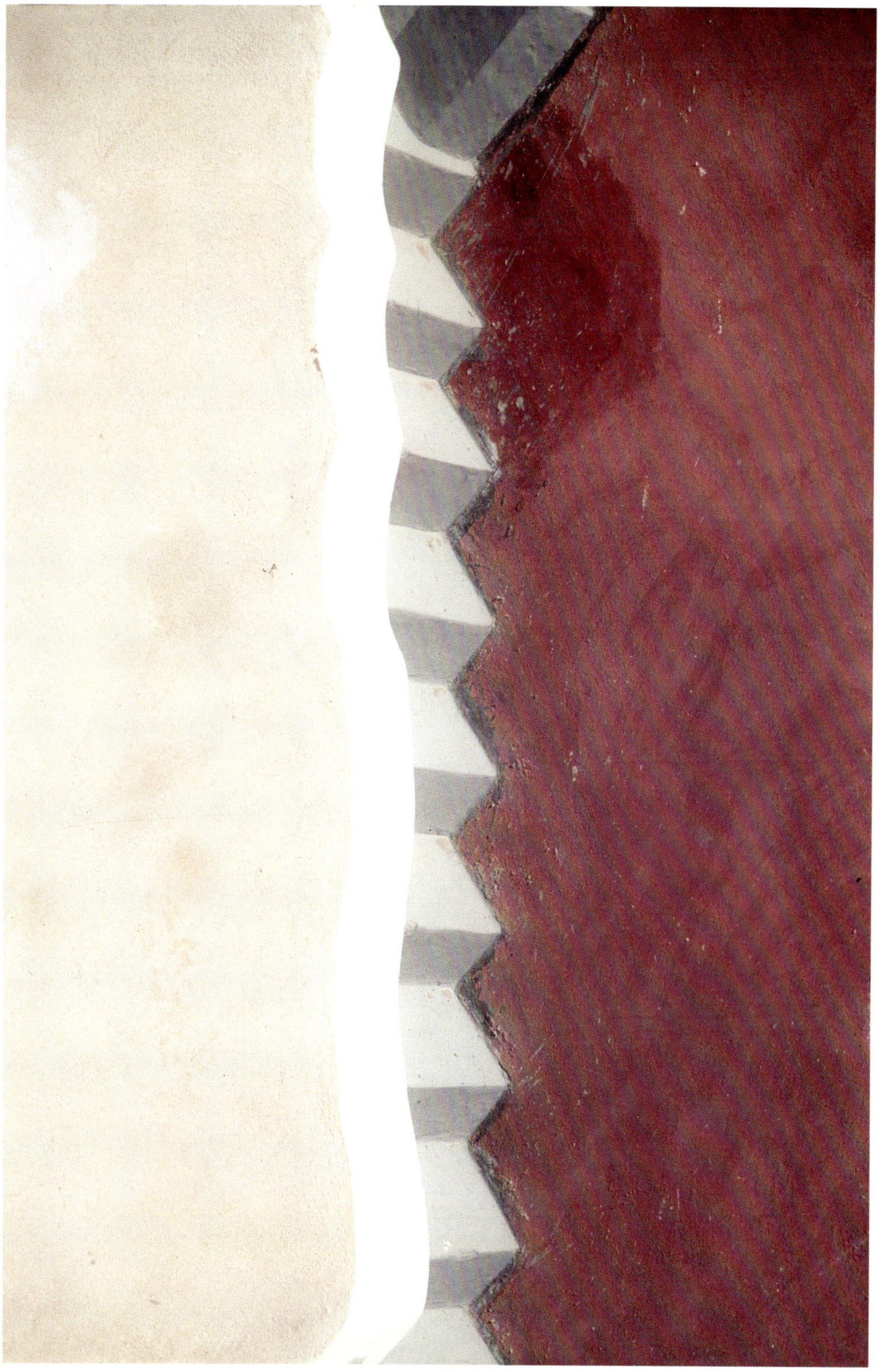

"Architecture is a language of metaphor."

James F. O'Gorman, writer

Red, White & Blue - 1

1996

Santorini

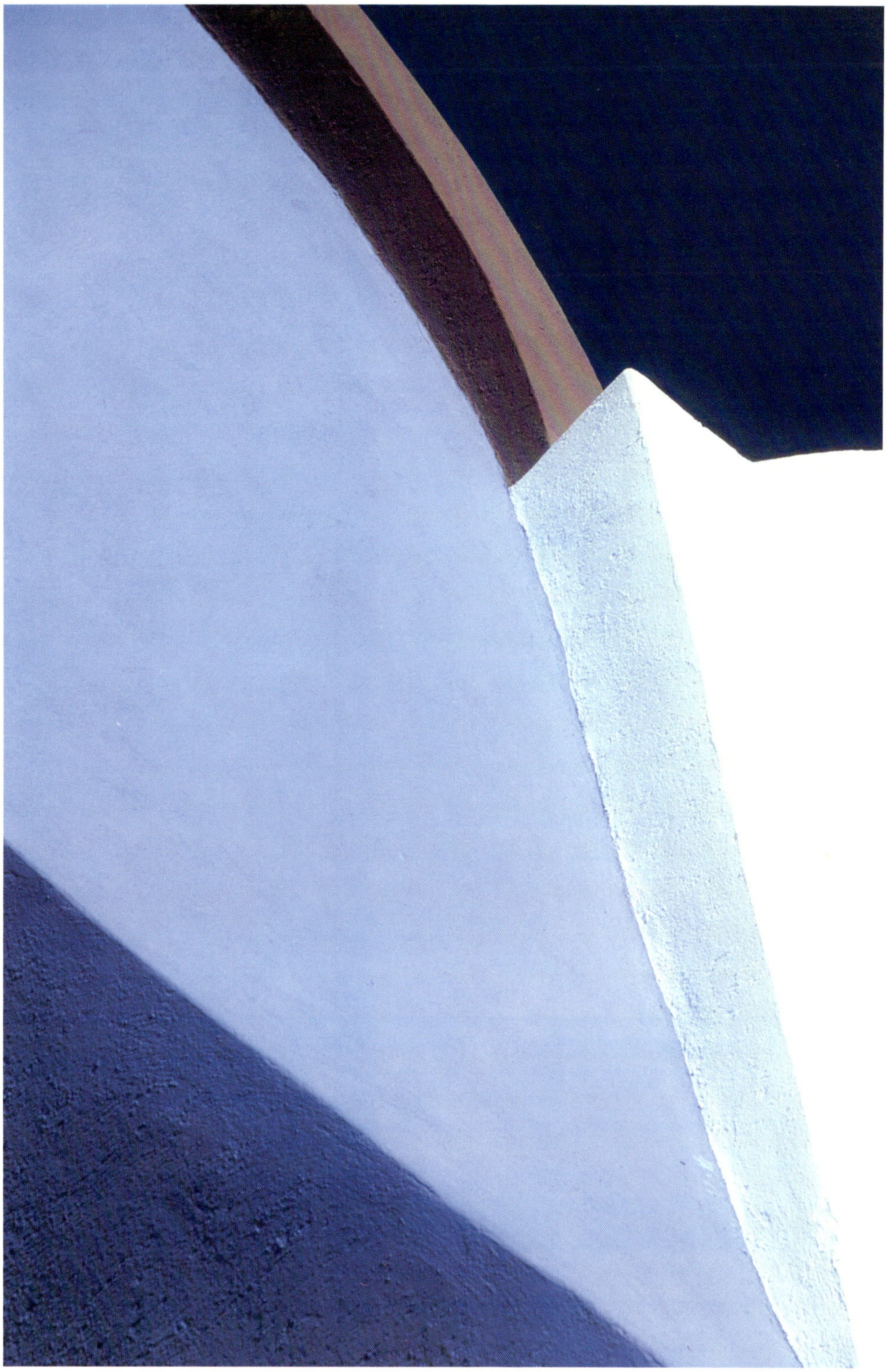

"Design gives the elements their shape, taking them from their existence in the mind to their tangible presence....In architecture, it characterizes a harmony of spaces good for a certain activity."

Louis I. Kahn, architect

Patch of Blue - 2

1996

Santorini

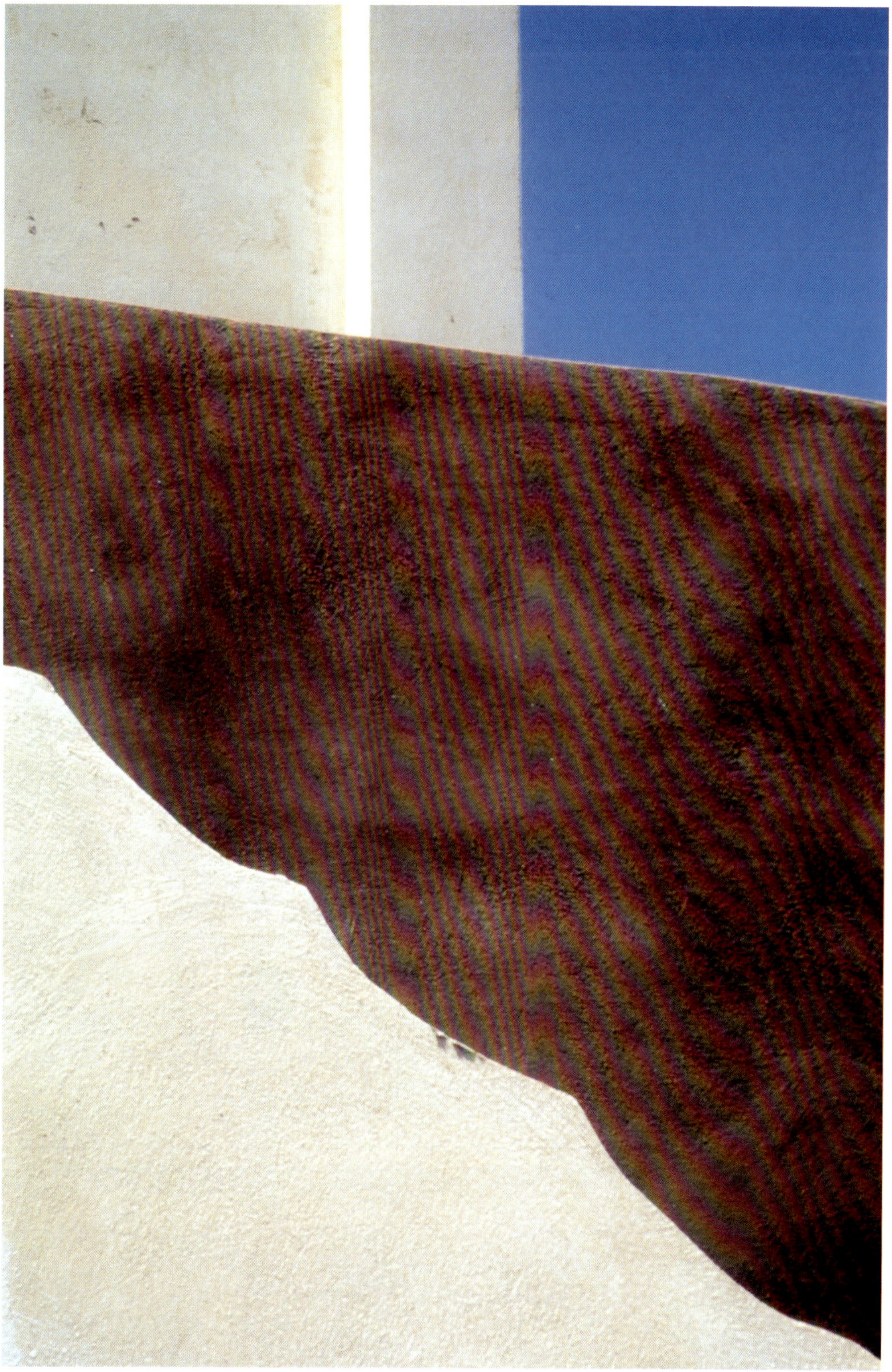

"Man creates to complement nature, and nature has its effects on man's creations."

I. M. Pei, architect

Earth-tone Stripes

1996

Santorini

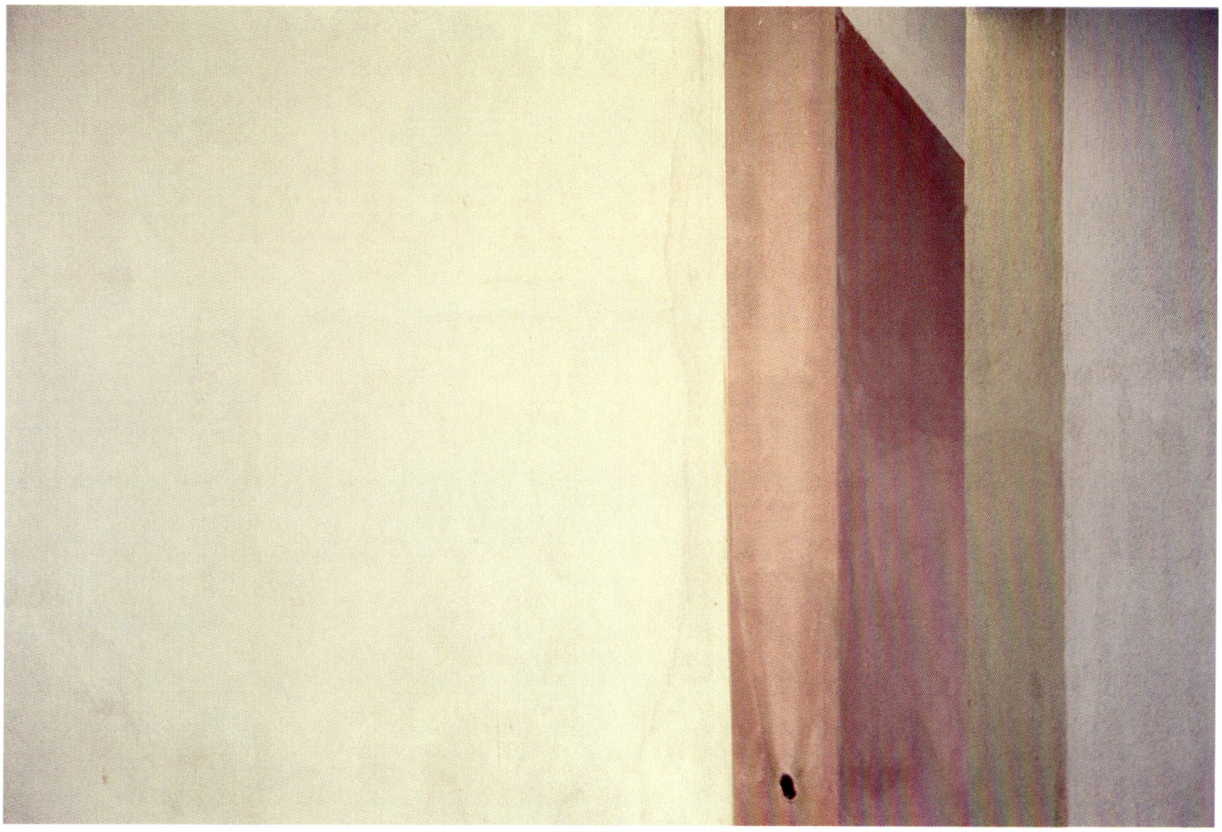

"... and this crumpled mass called material casts a shadow, and the shadow belongs to Light."

Louis I. Kahn, architect

Side Window
1996
Syros

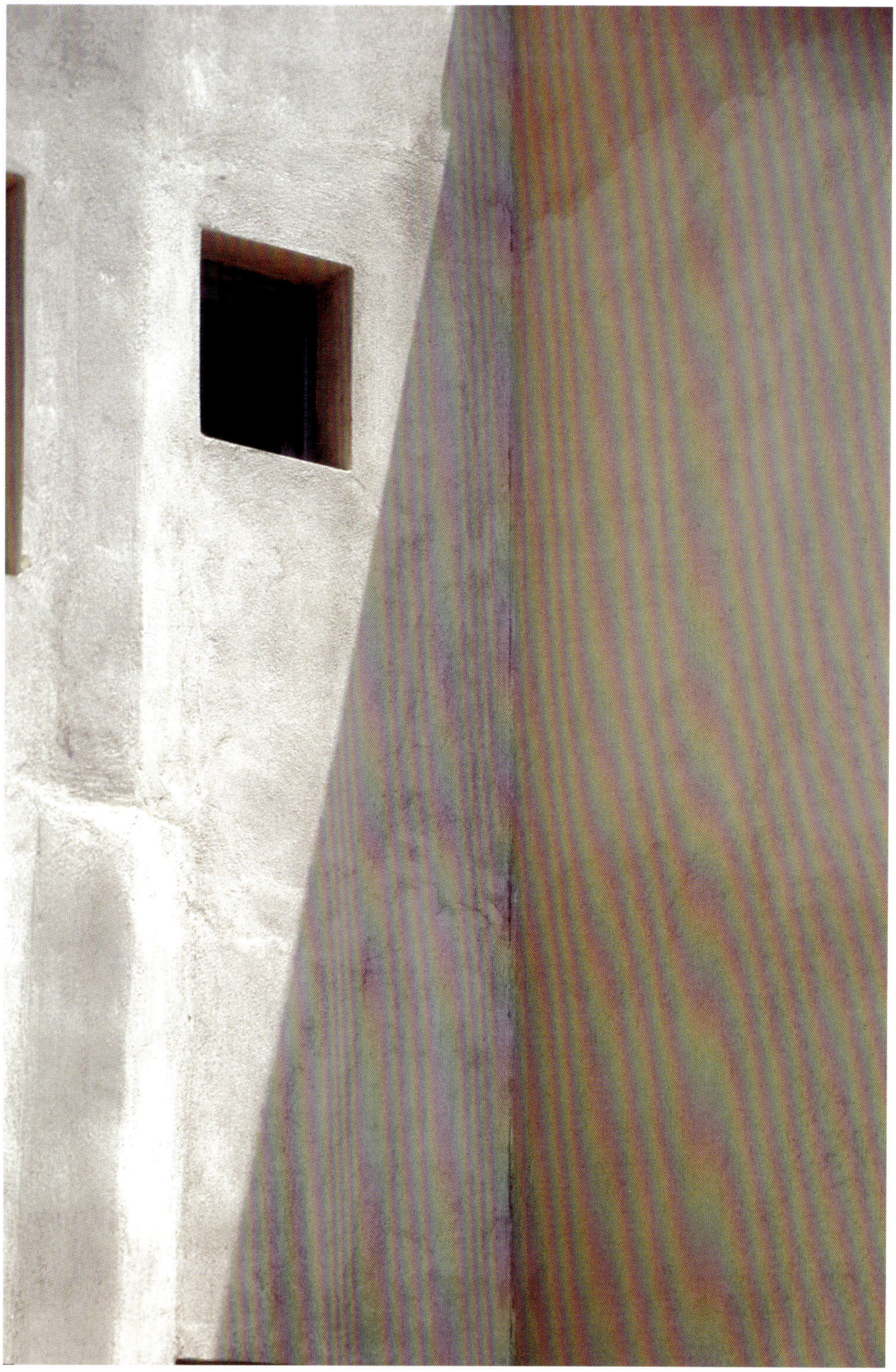

"I consider light, daylight especially, of fundamental importance to architecture. There is no space without light; there is no form without light. It is not an exaggeration to say that light is the key to architecture."

I. M. Pei, architect

White Arch

1996

Syros

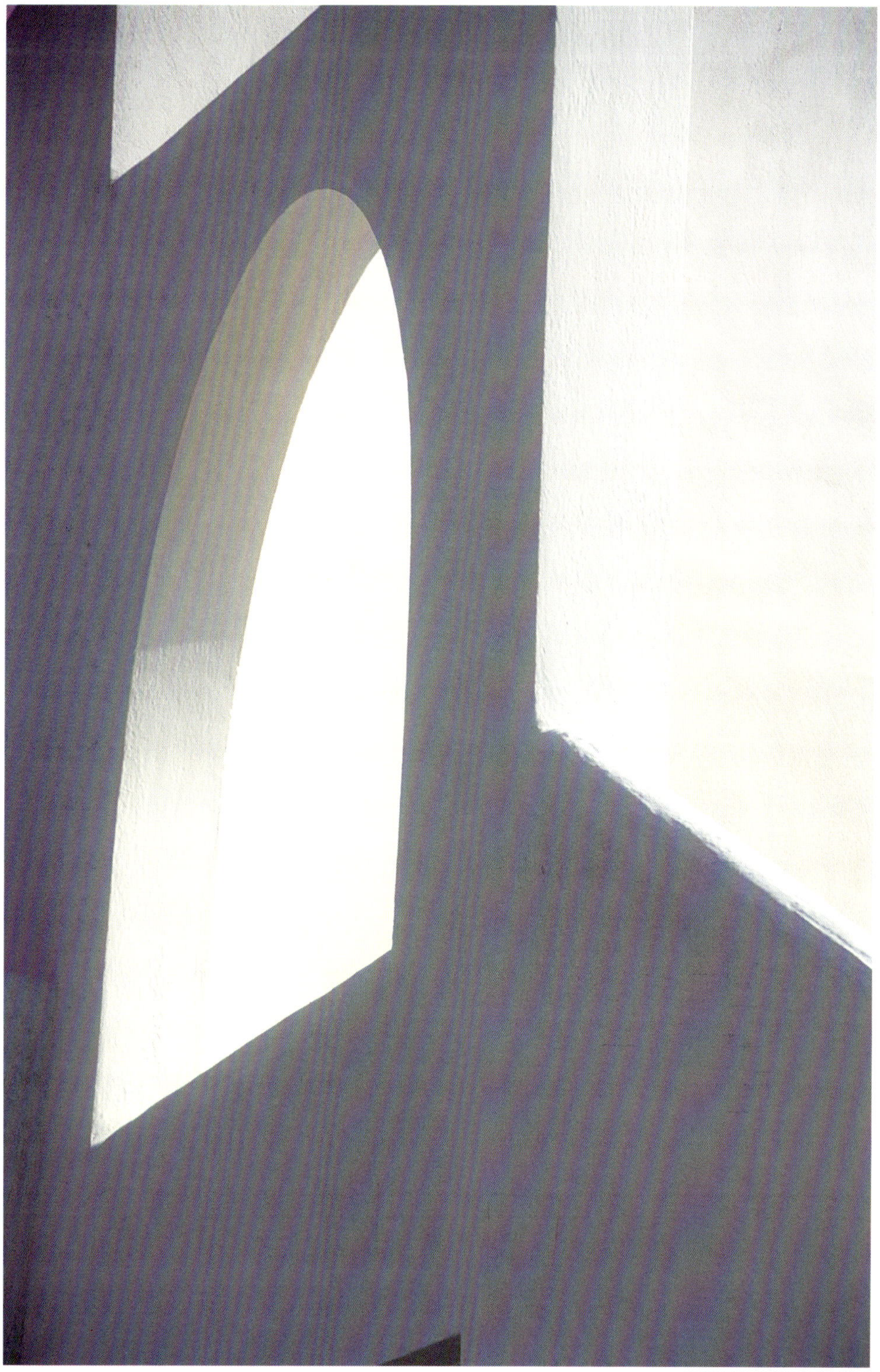

“The more a form is simplified, the more it clamors to be connected with a complex intellectual horizon.”

Pierre Schneider, writer

Light Hook
1996
Syros

“Light, the giver of presence, casts its shadow, which belongs to Light.”

Louis I. Kahn, architect

Keyhole Window

1996

Santorini

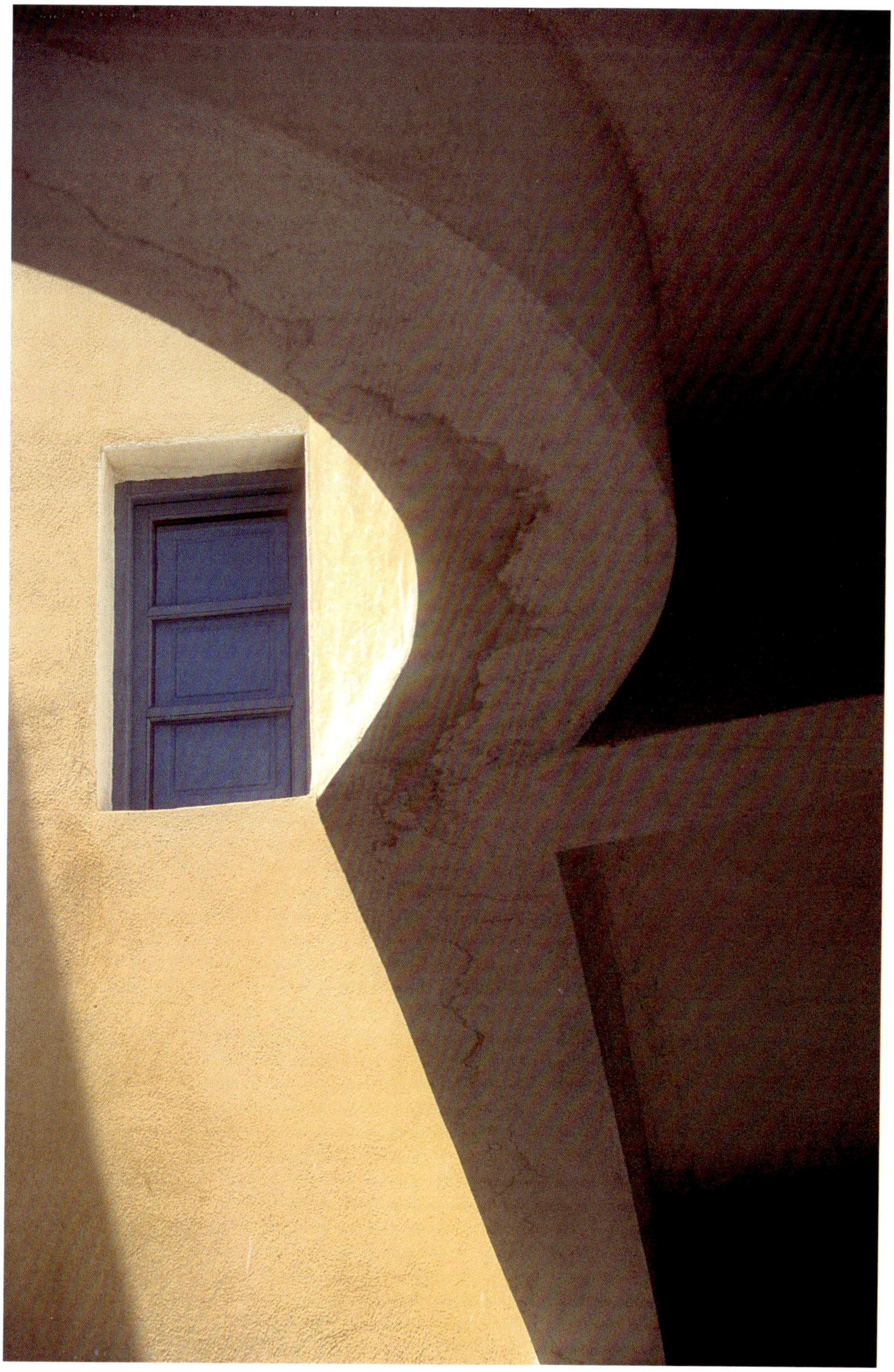

"The straight line belongs to man, the curve to God."

Antonio Gaudi, architect

Curve to Blue

1996

Syros

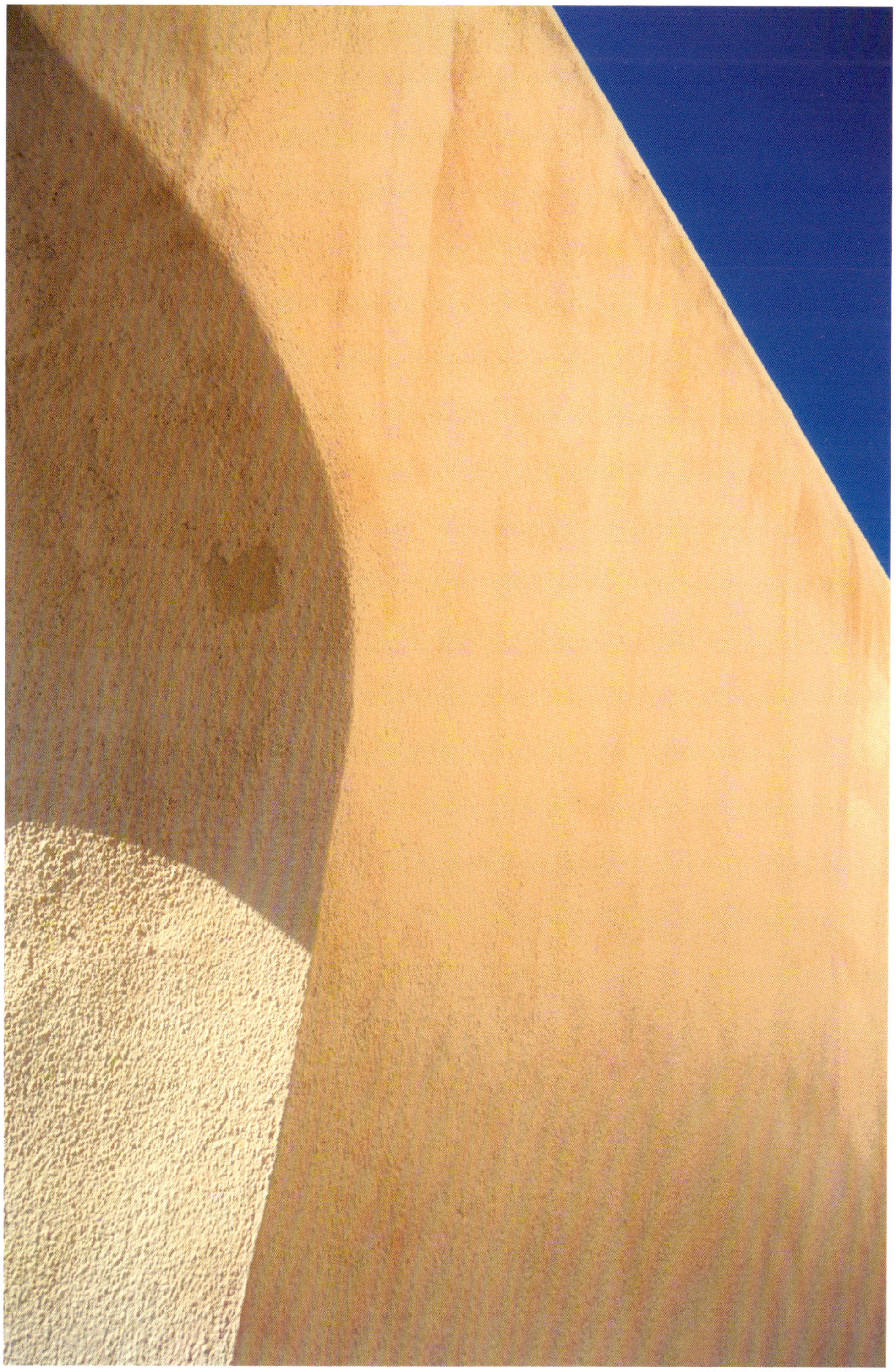

"Architecture has existence, but it has no presence. Only a work of architecture has presence, and a work of architecture is presented as an offering to architecture."

Louis I. Kahn, architect

Arch Puzzle - 1
1996
Santorini

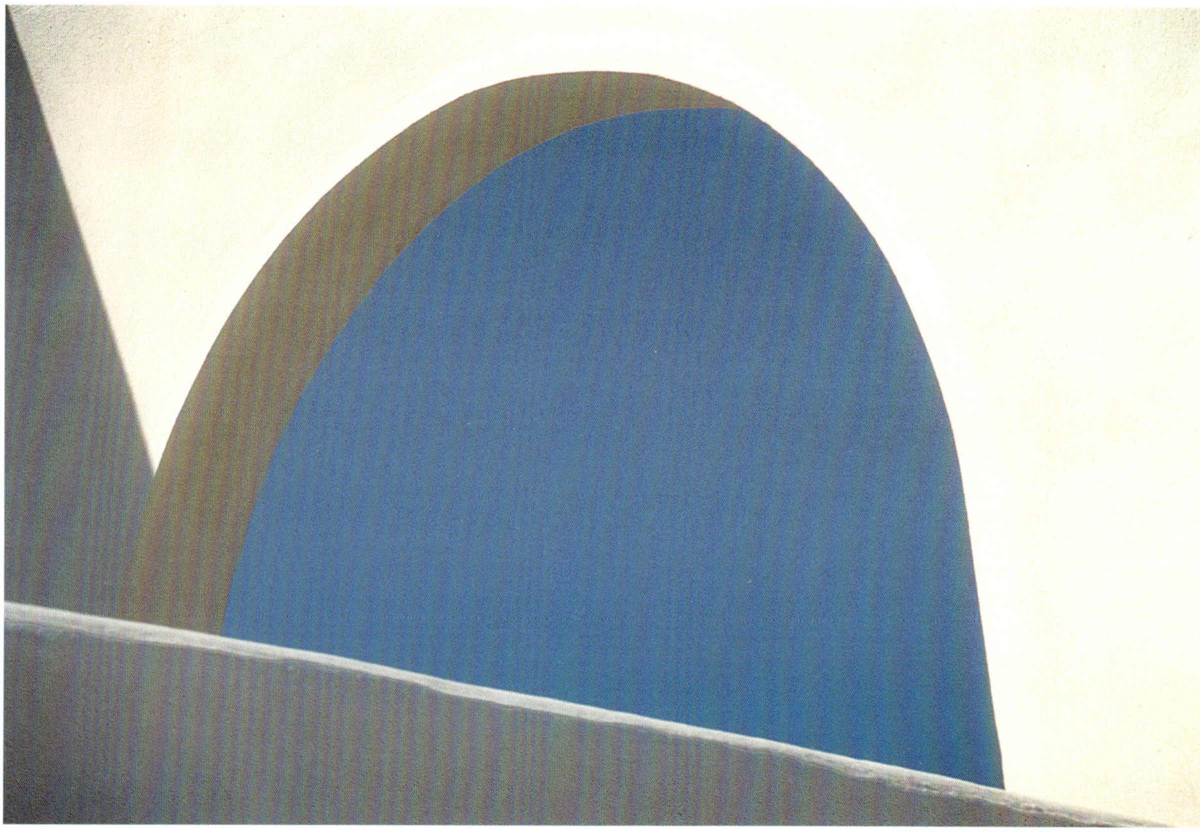

"Sun-treader, life and light be thine forever!"

Robert Browning, poet

White Stairway

1996

Santorini

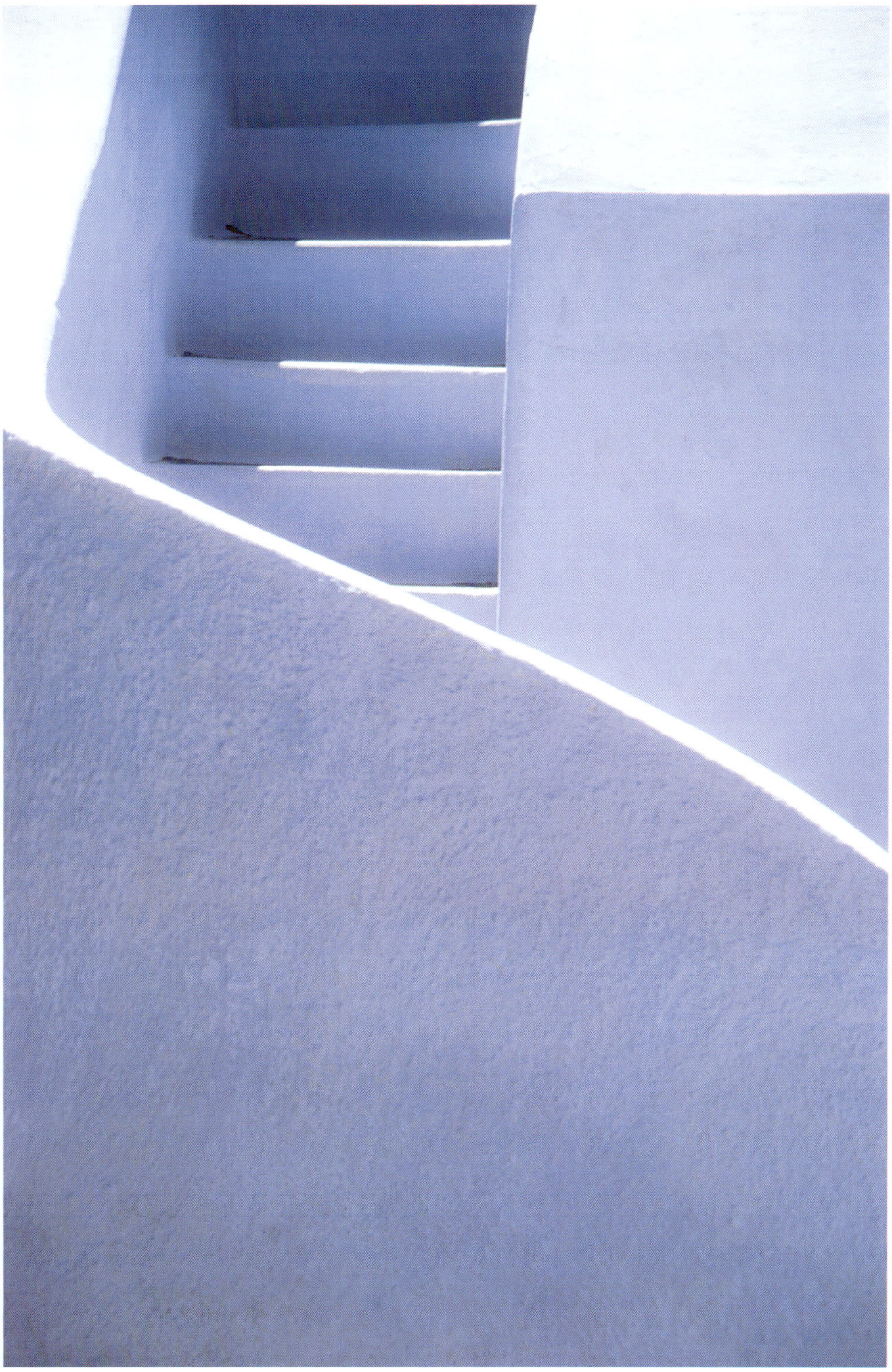

"Less is more."

Ludwig Mies van der Rohe, architect

Shutter Shade

1996

Santorini

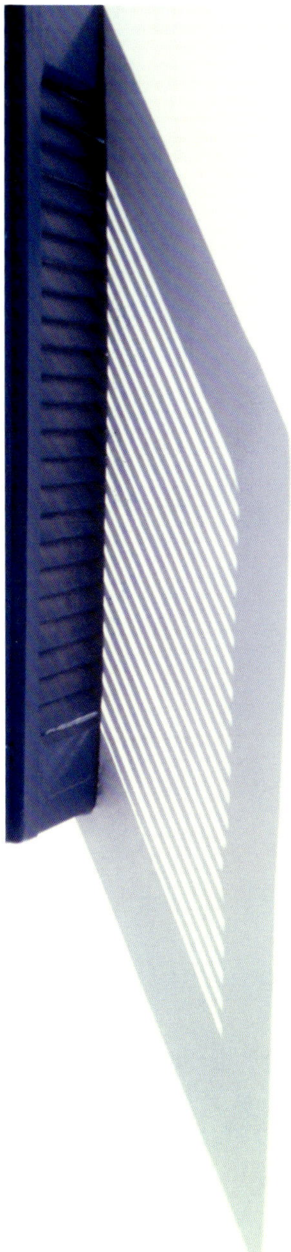

"Structure is the giver of light."

Louis I. Kahn, architect

Blue Herringbone

1996

Santorini

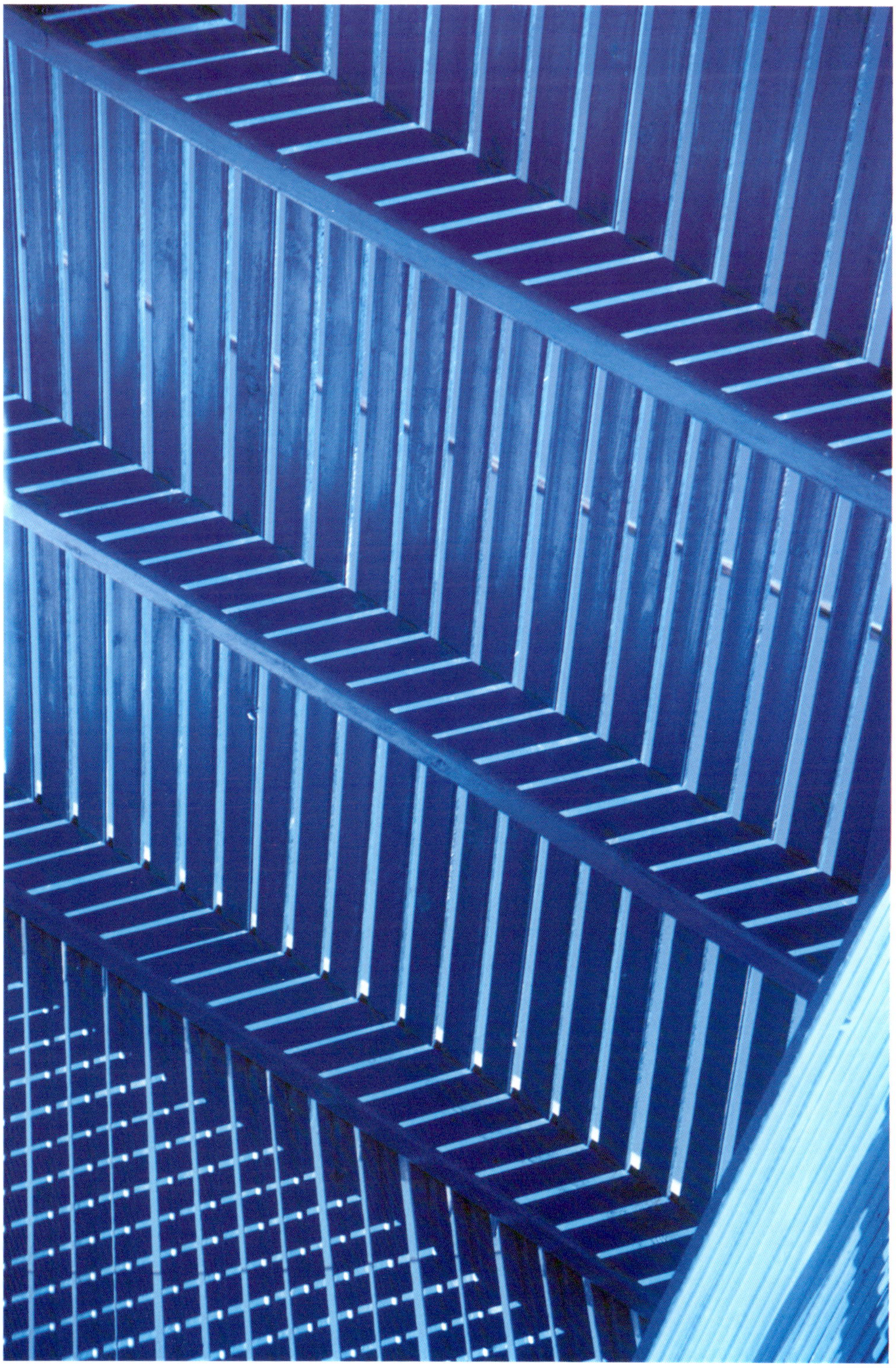

"If there is anything special in Greece, it is that special quality of light."

I. M. Pei, architect

Light Lines
1996
Santorini

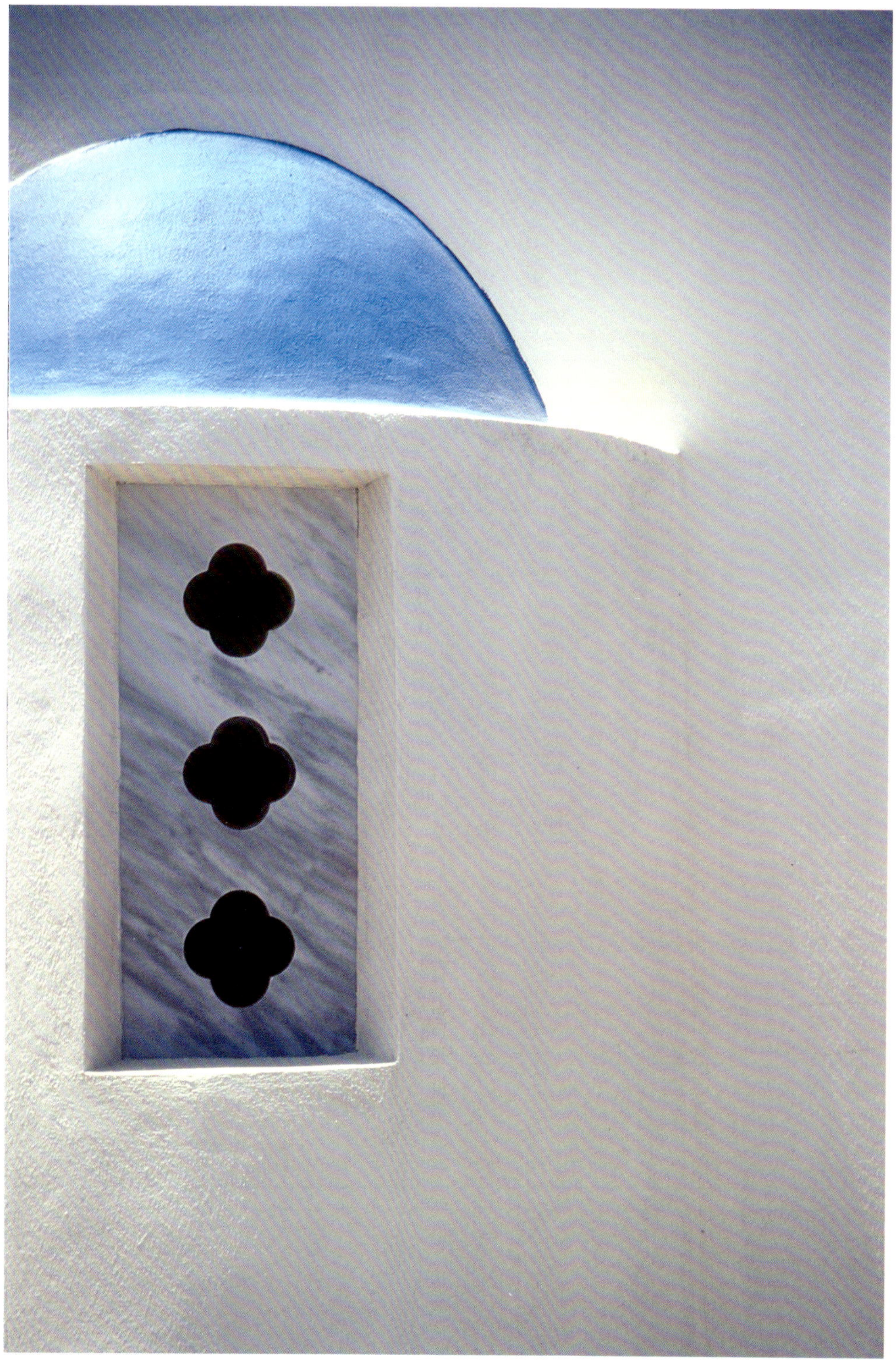

“Without the play of light, form is inert and space becomes static....”

I. M. Pei, architect

Sliver of Blue

1996

Syros

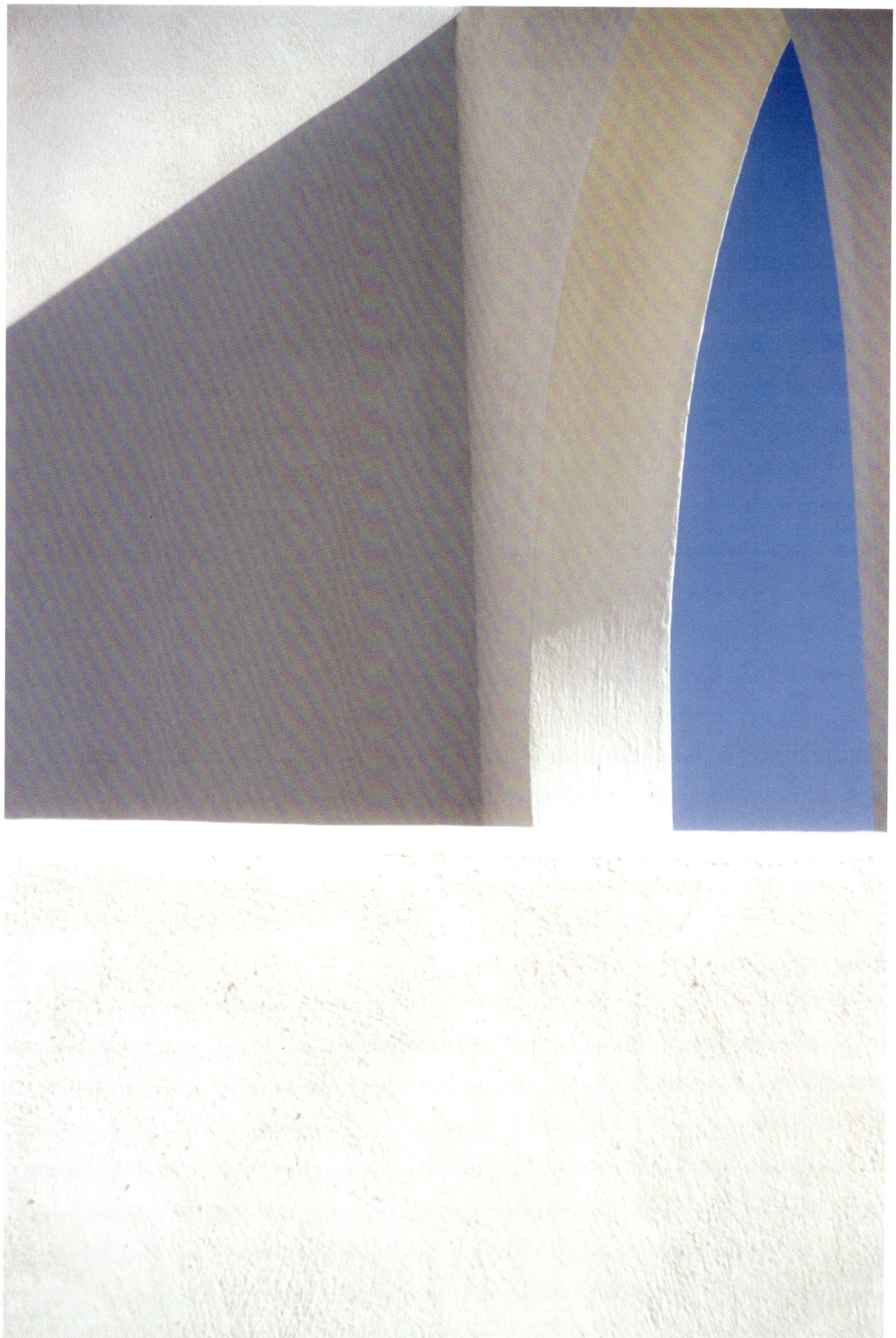

"But in the end, when the building becomes part of living, it evokes unmeasurable qualities, and the spirit of its existence takes over."

Louis I. Kahn, architect

Light Steps

1996

Mykonos

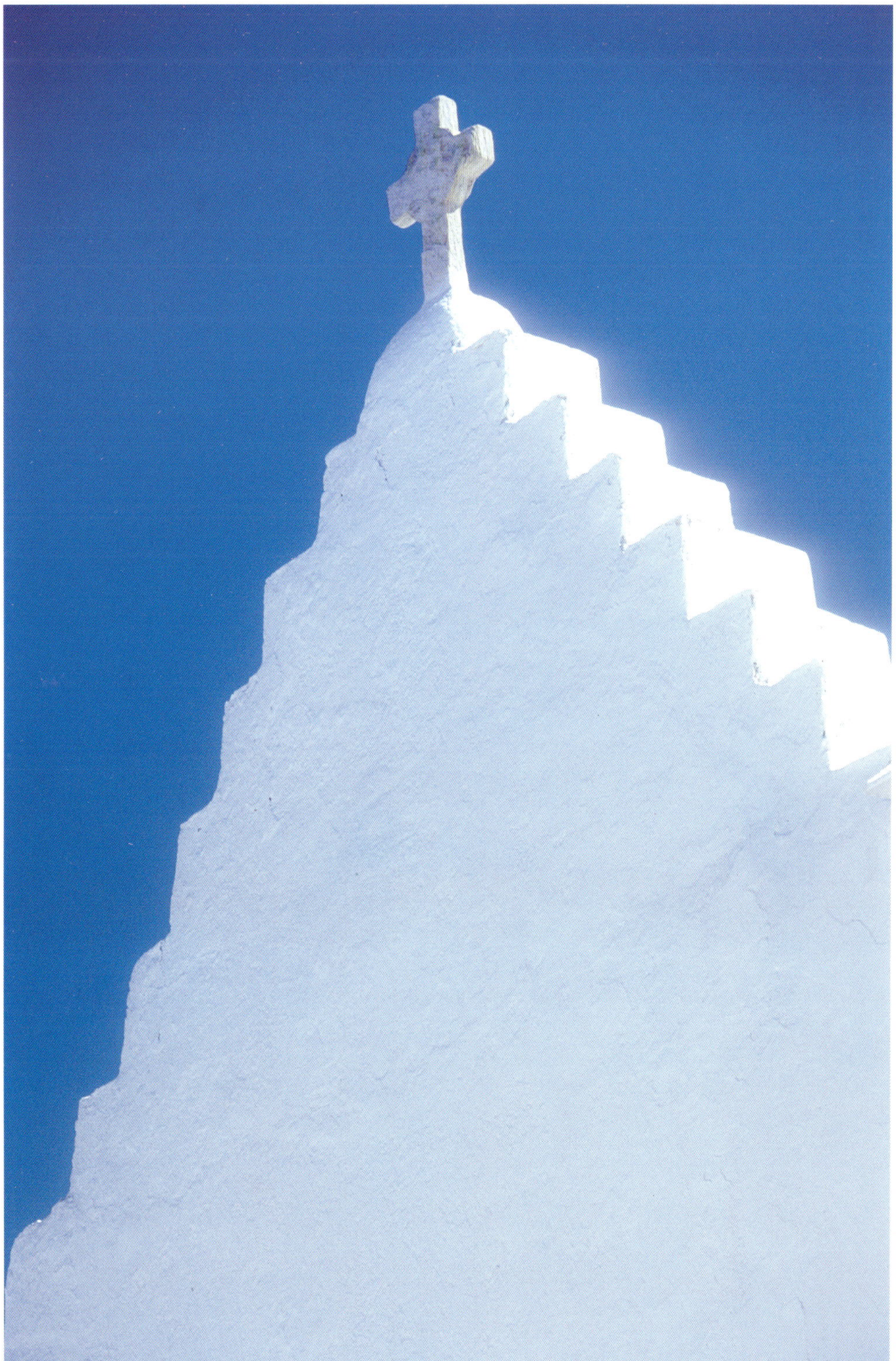

"Architecture is the learned game, correct and magnificent, of forms assembled in the light."

Le Corbusier, Swiss architect
and city planner

Patch of Blue - 1

1996

Santorini

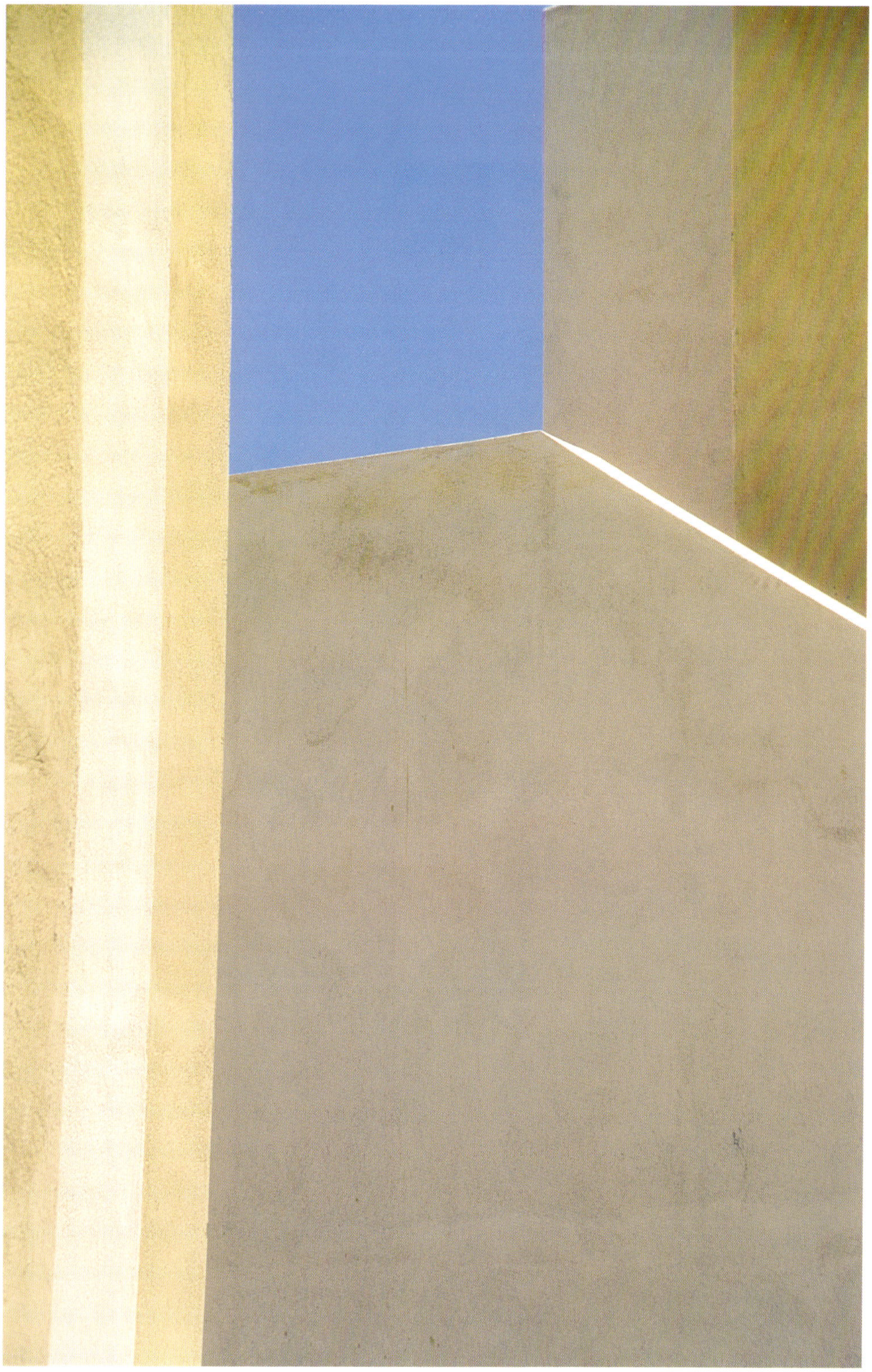

"Space has tonality, and I imagine myself composing a space lofty, vaulted, or under a dome, attributing to it a sound character alternating with the tones of space, narrow and high...light to darkness."

Louis I. Kahn, architect

Golden Arch

1996

Santorini

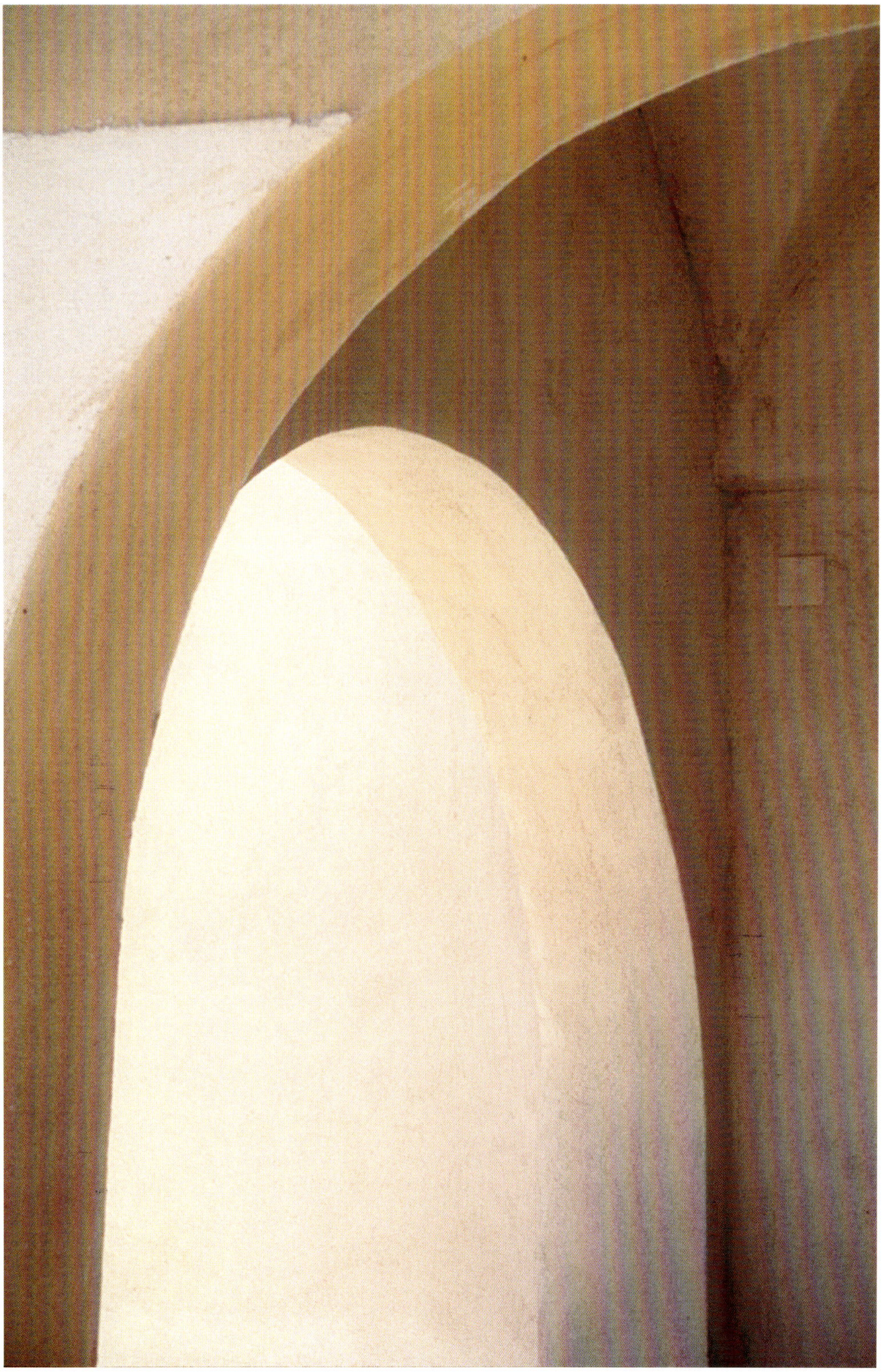

"Cats like free forms, changes of level, curves, angles, irregularity, and mixed materials. The white villages of the Cyclades suit them perfectly.... If architects paid more attention to the feelings of cats, we would live in much more pleasant homes."

Hans Silvester, photographer

Step Cat

1996

Syros

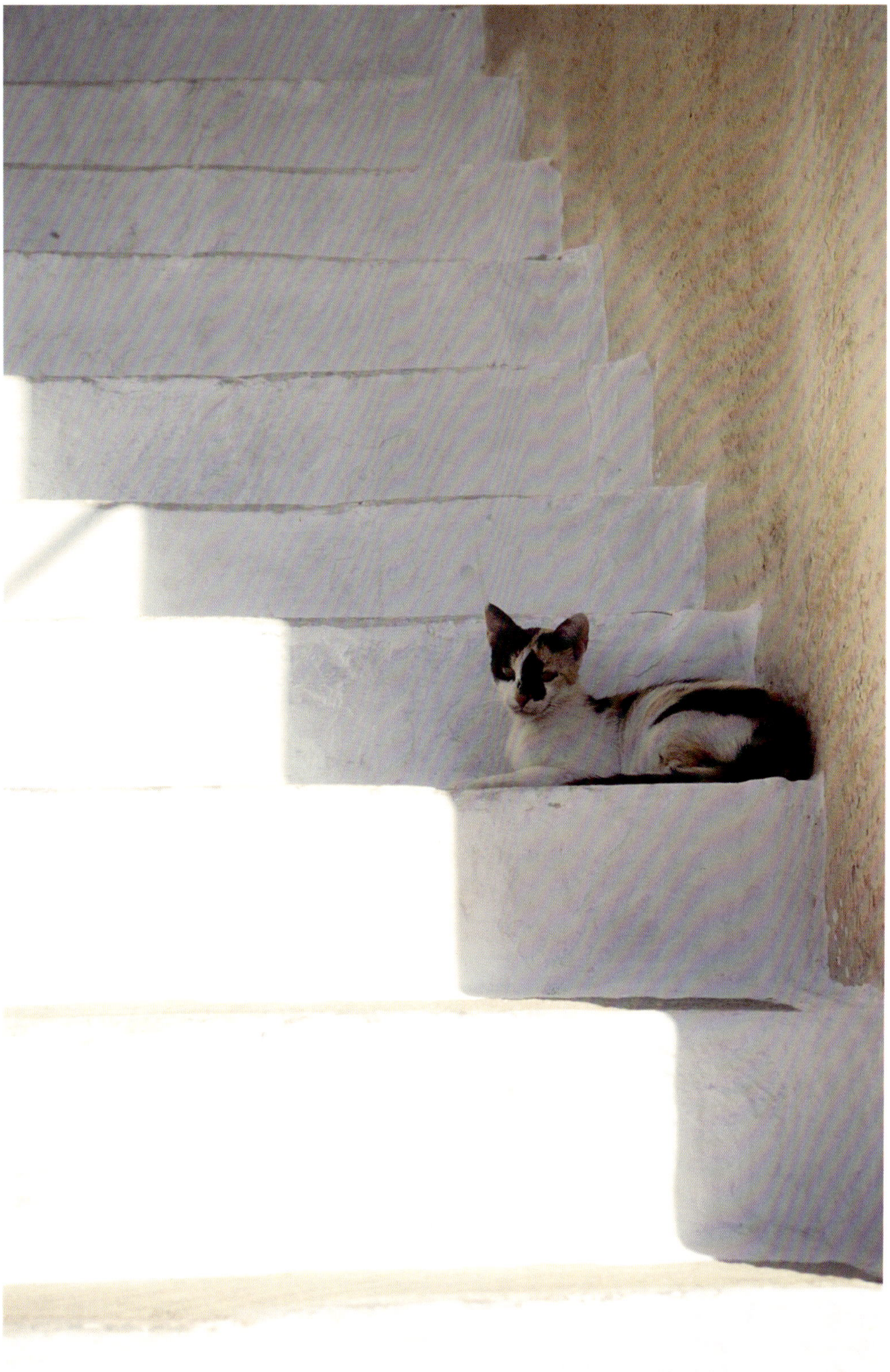

Notes about the images:

All of the images in this book are from Greece in the summer of 1996. Everyone in the group making the trip told me about the special quality of light in Greece, but I didn't understand it until I got there and saw it for myself.

The light in Greece is both beautiful and inspirational, and creates wonderful images from what Le Corbusier calls "forms assembled in the light." I have always been fascinated by architecture, and in that setting I got into something like a "zone" — very focused on light, form, shadow, texture, and the part of the total visual information that I found interesting.

Every day I was there I said to myself Robert Capa's credo: "If your pictures aren't good enough, you aren't close enough." Taking that advice, I tried to get closer to my subjects, and use the minimum amount of visual information to capture just the essence of the image. As Georgia O'Keeffe said, "...to see takes time..." and "It is only by selection, by elimination, by emphasis that we get at the real meaning of things."

At some level, I may have been looking for a more concise, focused, uncluttered message in an age of information overload. At some other level, these images may reflect my long time interest in the work of architect I. M. Pei and painter Georgia O'Keeffe. Mostly, though, I hope what shows through is that I was having a lot of fun, and I hope you enjoy looking at the results.

For all of these images, I used a Canon EOS 650, with a 35-105mm zoom lens. With one or two exceptions, the film was Fuji's Sensia or Provia. All images were shot using available light.

In print form, the images are Ilfochrome Deluxe Prints, and are in signed, limited editions of 25. The usual print sizes (image areas) are 11"x 14", and 16"x 20", but are also available in smaller sizes. The images are printed full frame, with no manipulation by any digital process nor any enhancement by computer software.

Carolyn Johnson
July 2002

Carolyn Johnson
Photographer

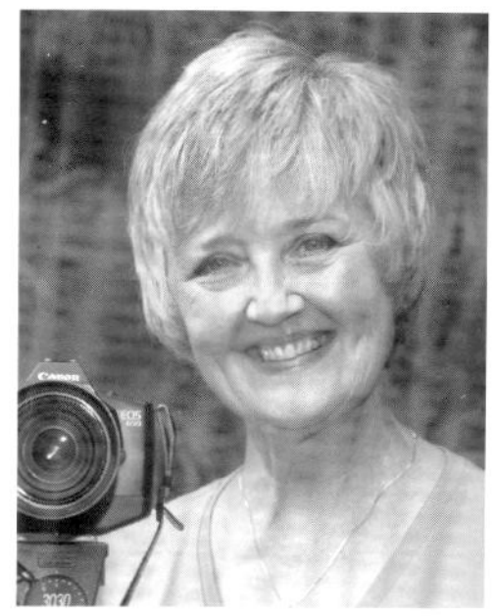

Carolyn Johnson has worked as a photographer in Washington, D.C., over the last twelve years. She has studied photography both in the U.S. and abroad, including at the Corcoran School of Art and the Smithsonian Institution in Washington, D.C., at Glen Echo Park in Maryland, and independently with Washington photographer Charles Rumph. Her B.A. is in Spanish, with studies at the University of Oklahoma and the University of Madrid. Her M.S. is in Computer Systems and MIS from American University in Washington, D.C.

Her early work in black and white included theatre photography, some of which was published in *The Washington Post*. Over the last several years, Ms. Johnson began to work in color. Along with that change, she developed a strong interest in architectural images and these have dominated her exhibited work.

Ms. Johnson has exhibited her work in group shows — both juried and by-invitation — at the World Bank and the International Monetary Fund in Washington, D.C., and the Glenview Mansion Art Gallery in Rockville, Maryland. In addition, she has had five solo exhibitions in corporate gallery space in the Washington, D.C., area.

Ms. Johnson's recent and current exhibition schedule is shown below:

- **January - July 2001**, The MITRE Corporation in McLean, Virginia, hosted a solo exhibition of images from southern France.
- **April - June 2001**, the Embassy of Greece in Washington, D.C., exhibited a collection of her architectural images from Greece.
- **June 7 - August 3, 2001**, the American Architectural Foundation hosted a solo exhibition of her work from Greece at the American Institute of Architects Headquarters Gallery in Washington, D.C.
- **December 2001**, the Plains Indians & Pioneers Museum in Oklahoma hosted a solo exhibition of her work from southern France.
- **July-December 2002, The** American Institute of Architects is displaying a collection of her images from southern france.
- **August 2002**, the Glenview Mansion Art Gallery in Rockville, Maryland, will host a solo exhibition of her work from Greece.

For more information, please visit the studio: www.carolynjohnsonstudio.com